The Emotional Life of Contemporary Public

The Emotional Life of Contemporary Public Memorials
Towards a Theory of Temporary Memorials

Erika Doss

AMSTERDAM UNIVERSITY PRESS

The Meertens Ethnology Cahiers are revised texts of the Meertens Ethnology Lectures. These lectures are presented by ground-breaking researchers in the field of ethnology and related disciplines at the Meertens Institute in Amsterdam, a research facility in language and culture in the Netherlands

The Meertens Institute is a research institute of the Royal Netherlands Academy of Arts and Sciences

Meertens Institute
Department of Ethnology
PO Box 94264
1090 GG Amsterdam
www.meertens.knaw.nl

Meertens Ethnology Cahier iii
Series Editor: Peter Jan Margry
peter.jan.margry@meertens.knaw.nl

Illustration front cover: Temporary memorial created in September 2001 featuring a teddy bear and flowers at the Pentagon, Arlington, VA. Photo Erika Doss. Photo back cover: P.J. Margry

Cover design: Kok Korpershoek, Amsterdam
Lay out: JAPES, Amsterdam

ISBN   978 90 8964 018 5
ISSN   1872-0986

© Amsterdam University Press, 2008

In 1976, the Eakins Press Foundation published *The American Monument*, an oversize volume featuring 213 photographs taken by Lee Friedlander of the commemorative landscape of the United States: the memorials, statues, and shrines occupying America's parks, squares, cemeteries, and public spaces. While many of Friedlander's images of Pilgrim mothers, town fathers, Sons of Liberty, U.S. presidents, Civil War heroes, and volunteer fireman were sly and even humorous – with some of his shots of lonely statues and cluttered urban landscapes revealing the neglect of posterity, the litter of modernity *The American Monument* largely reflected the faith that Americans place in material culture to mediate their histories and memories. Memorials 'embody the idea of excellences worthy of permanence,' the book's editor concluded, adding: 'Monuments are metaphors for human values, persistent values that survive despite notice or neglect, unaccounted for by computers, cynicism, or professions of piety.'[1]

The past few decades have witnessed a veritable explosion of public monument-making in the United States and Europe, but of a kind and purpose significantly different from that of previous generations. Indeed, a major shift has taken place in contemporary commemorative culture: from the monument to the memorial; from the monolithic master narratives of 'official' art to the diverse, subjective, and often conflicted expressions of multiple publics. In contrast to the ennobling, authoritative, and pious monuments of the past, today's memorials are especially disposed to individual memories and personal grievances, and often attuned to tragic and traumatic historical episodes and eras. Consider the Memorial for the Murdered Jews of Europe, dedicated in Berlin in 2005, and the New England Holocaust Memorial, dedicated in Boston in 1997. The Netherlands also features a number of Holocaust memorials, including the Nooit Meer Auschwitz ('Never Again Auschwitz') Monument, designed by Jan Wolkers and dedicated in Amsterdam's Wertheim Park in 1993, and the Homomonument (the first memorial honoring gays and lesbians killed during the Nazi Holocaust), which was designed by Karin Daan and dedicated along Amsterdam's Prinsengracht, near the Anne Frank Museum, in 1987. In 2002, the Slavernij Monument, commemorating the victims of slavery in the Netherlands, was dedicated in Amsterdam's Oosterpark.

Likewise, the Netherlands has seen its share of temporary memorials: those ephemeral memorials made of flowers, candles, balloons, hand-penned letters, sympathy cards, and stuffed animals that precipitate after unexpected, and generally highly-publicized, traumas, often on the site where those traumas have occurred. Following the murders of controversial Dutch politician Pim Fortuyn in 2002, and similarly controversial Dutch filmmaker Theo Van Gogh in 2004, the outdoor sites were they were slain (and sites elsewhere) became temporary shrine sites decorated with votive candles, floral tributes, cards, posters, photographs, teddy bears, and other offerings particular to their personalities and those of their mourners. Following 9/11, the exterior grounds of the U.S. Embassy in The Hague were literally blanketed with bouquets of flowers, cards, and candles. Temporary memorials were also erected after the 1996 Hercules disaster, in which a military transport plane crashed and left thirty-four dead in Eindhoven, in the southern Netherlands; after the 2000 explosion in a fireworks factory in Enschede, in which twenty-two people died; and after the 2001 New Year's Day fire in Volendam, a small village north of Amsterdam, that claimed the lives of fourteen people.[2] And while it is mostly mass disaster and mass-mediated tragedy that commands large-scale, national attention in the Netherlands (as in other nations), roadside memorials – those hand-made crosses that are erected by grieving families and friends at the sites of fatal traffic accidents, and are often decorated with flowers, personal items, and photos – can be seen throughout the country, and elsewhere around the world.

Temporary memorial for the murdered Dutch politician Pim Fortuyn, created at the basement of the statue of the father of the nation, William the Silent († 1584), May 2002. Photo Peter Jan Margry.

If wildly divergent in subject and style – few of today's memorials hold to the classicizing sentiments of earlier generations – these commemorative sites collectively represent what I call 'memorial mania': the contemporary obsession with issues of memory and history and an urgent, excessive desire to express, or claim, those issues in visibly public contexts.[3] Contemporary acts, rituals, or performances of memorialization are often exorbitant, frenzied, and extreme – or manic. Their pathos and inconstancy are not surprising: memory itself is often unpredictable and unstable, and rituals of memorialization are often prompted by emotional states of being such as grief, guilt, and gratitude. Furthermore, contemporary modes of commemoration are visibly marked by conflict, rupture, and loss: by a recognition among diverse publics that memorials have the power to stir things up as much as they may smooth them out.

This essay proposes a theoretically attuned consideration of one form, or variety, of contemporary memorialization: that of temporary memorials, and the impromptu and instantaneous performances of public commemoration that they seemingly represent. It argues that their meaning lies especially in their affective dimensions, and particularly in their cultural negotiation of public grief. As such, their contextualization is highly dependent on contemporary understandings of memory, mourning, and public feeling.

The subject is confounded by the problem of definitions, and the manner in which particular terms shape and direct the meaning of (and assumptions about) these kinds of commemoration.[4] Some writers use the term 'temporary memorials' to distinguish them from permanent forms of commemoration; others call them 'vernacular memorials' to differentiate them as individual, localized, and grassroots responses, rather than officially sanctioned or institutionalized projects. Some refer to them as 'performative memorials' to explicate their fundamentally active and social nature.[5] Some use the terms 'spontaneous memorials' and 'spontaneous shrines' to emphasize their seemingly abrupt and unpremeditated appearance, and to reference the religious items and images they often include.

But any nomenclature does well to remember that these memorials are mercurial by nature: they may originate as ephemeral forms and sites of commemoration but as they are photographed and collected (increasingly, the objects of many temporary memorials are saved and stored), they enter into new taxonomic registers. Likewise, the formulaic and increasingly universalized nature of their production calls into question their vernacular sensibility. By extension, the use of the term 'spontaneous' is a misnomer: however impromptu, these memorials are highly orchestrated and self-conscious performances of mourning, rituals of public lamentation aimed at expressing, codifying, and ultimately managing grief. Their spontaneity is only in their origination, in their swift response to the sudden and unexpected events of tragic and traumatic death. While the term 'spontaneous shrine' has a certain charming alliteration, it generally bears little relation to the scripted and often secular dimensions of these particular kinds of commemoration.[6]

Given this, I opt for the term 'temporary memorials,' recognizing that what we are especially considering is the cultural production and consumption of ephemeral forms of commemoration, some of which are eventually transformed to become permanent and institutionalized memorials. Grappling with the emotional conditions that underlie the making and meaning of these memorials, this discussion focuses especially on their processual nature: on how they are produced, seen, experienced, and made meaningful. In this regard, commemoration is understood as both the site of symbolic activity and of organized (or what can be determined as organized) human experience. Memorials are visual, material, intellectual, and emotional bodies; hence, their social, cultural, and political meanings cannot be derived without a simultaneous appreciation of their affective nuances.

The literature on temporary memorials is substantial, and mostly focused on a case study methodology integral to anthropological and ethnographic practices.[7] Indeed, the term 'spontaneous memorials' was originally coined by folklorist Jack Santino in a 1992 essay on murder sites in Northern Ireland that had become shrine sites: places visited by the families and supporters of victims of political assassination; places physically transformed by their gifts of flowers, notes, and other objects; places accorded special, even sacred, status by the ritualized acts and offerings of everyday urban pilgrims.[8] Following on the work of linguist John L. Austin, Santino has since refined his initial thoughts on these public displays, arguing for their conceptualization as 'performative commemoratives' that mark instances of untimely and especially traumatic deaths, become places of communion between the living and dead, and invite broad public participation. As he observes, spontaneous memorials 'display death in the heart of social life. These are not graves awaiting occasional visitors and sanctioned decorations. Instead of a family visiting a grave, the 'grave' comes to the family – that is, the public. All of us.'[9]

Recent scholarship on temporary memorials similarly argues that these public displays of death provide evidence of civic and communal practices that are separate and distinct from official, or mainstream, commemorative practices. Such memorials are believed to constitute acts and places of social agency, and even social challenge. As art historian Harriet Senie remarks, 'Spontaneous memorials are populist phenomena, ways for people to mark their own history. They create a public place for individuals and communities united in grief and often anger.'[10]

Temporary memorials to Princess Diana in front of Kensington Palace, London, September 1997. Photo Robert and Vicky Wright.

Examples abound, including the international array of temporary memorials created after the death of Princess Diana on August 31, 1997. Dubbed 'The People's Princess' by newly-elected British Prime Minister Tony Blair, Diana's unexpected death in a car accident generated an equally unexpected outpouring of public grief, represented in the vast sea of flowers, handwritten notes, and other offerings that emerged in front of Kensington Palace (her official London residence), Buckingham Palace (the Queen's London residence), and in many smaller, if no less deeply felt, tributes to her all over the world, including several in the Netherlands. Many have discussed the public mourning of Diana's death on oppositional terms, as evidence of populist and politically motivated expressions of grief that signaled strains of collective civic protest. Santino, for example, describes the temporary memorials erected to Diana in London as a kind of 'cultural-political contestation' to the elite trappings of the British royal family; others have likened them as a 'floral revolution': a popular grassroots uprising against the policing of mourning in modern Great Britain, and a populist demand for inclusion in a bounded and class-divided society.[11]

There is no doubt that temporary memorials represent changed cultural and social practices regarding public mourning, if initial claims that they represent *new* practices have been countenanced by the ongoing scholarly recovery of their origins and histories.[12] Temporary memorials may not be especially new but they are, I believe, becoming more widespread as the phenomenon of 'memorial mania' continues. As manifest in their materialist forms and emotional conditions, these practices of public mourning suggest that 'traditional' forms of mourning do not meet the needs of today's publics, which prompts questions about what death, grief, and memory mean in the new millennium. More specifically: how are feelings of grief mediated in contemporary temporary memorials? What role do emotions play in the making and meaning of these memorials, and what roles do these memorials play in the fabrication of individual and public subjectivity? What do these memorial practices tell us about who, and what, is deemed memorable in contemporary historical consciousness?

Memorials, I argue, are the physical and visual embodiment of public affect. They are, to paraphrase Ann Cvektovich, a public 'archive of feelings' and as such can be considered 'repositories of feelings and emotions' which are encoded not only in their material form and narrative content but also 'in the practices that surround their production and reception.'[13] Interests in 'understanding the cultural dimensions of sensory perception have been rising since the 1980s', observes Regina Bendix, and the challenge for anthropologists and other scholars is to integrate these sensory and affective dimensions 'into the overall ethnographic project.' As Lauren Berlant argues, the complex circulation of emotions, and the broader sociocultural and sociopolitical implications of this 'sensual turn,' demand a 'critical realm of the senses' that considers 'what feelings are made out to mean; and which forces, meanings, and practices are magnetized by concepts of affect and emotion.'[14]

Affect – Frederick Jameson notwithstanding – is omnipresent in contemporary America. Contrary to a Habermasian vision of a rational and collective public sphere in which sensible citizens exchange ideas and unite in progressive action, contemporary public life is marked by emotional appeals and affective conditions: consider how public feelings have been mobilized and manipulated in recent political elections, in ongoing debates over issues of abortion and reproductive rights, and over the 'war on terror.' These affective dimensions do not foreclose the possibilities of social and political transformation. But they do beg for a critical pedagogy of public feelings – an emotional epistemology – which recognizes how and why (and which) feelings shape historical moments, concepts of citizenship, and understandings of self and national identity.

Things Matter

As material culture theorists from Jules Prown to Daniel Miller argue, 'things matter,' and the fact that many people have made temporary memorials a priority among their many diverse 'object worlds' matters a great deal.[15] The palpable stuff of which they are made both describes and defines them; temporary memorials are in many ways exemplars of Pierre Nora's observation that 'modern memory is, above all, archival.'[16] In September 1997, an estimated 15,000 tons of flowers and other offerings formed the temporary memorials created at London's royal palaces in memory of Princess Diana. In Littleton, Colorado in 1999, over 200,000 items were left at the huge memorial that developed after the shootings at Columbine High School, in which fifteen people were killed. In Oklahoma City, Oklahoma, perhaps as many as one million items were left on Memory Fence, an eight-foot tall chain-link fence that circled the large area formerly occupied by the Murrah Federal Building, which Timothy McVeigh

Temporary memorial at Columbine High School, Littleton, CO, 1999.
Photo Erika Doss.

bombed in April 1995, killing 168 people. Built immediately after the bombing to restrict public access to the crime scene, Memory Fence became covered in 'tokens of remembrance', including stuffed animals, plastic flowers, laminated poems, hand-drawn pictures, military medals, and religious mementos that were left by thousands of visitors from 1995-2000 (when a permanent memorial was dedicated on the site). Local residents who lost family and friends in the bombing claimed particular areas of the fence and added personal belongings including toys, photographs, baby blankets, and prom flowers. Tourists visiting the site either prepared offerings in advance or added items closest at hand when they arrived at the site, including their t-shirts or hats, onto which they often inscribed their names, the dates of their visit, and sentiments such as 'We Remember, We Will Never Forget.'[17]

Links between material culture and mourning are timeless, of course, and the rituals of gift-giving at temporary memorials obviously stem from longstanding materialist practices that serve to memorialize the dead. Rituals of death abound in materialism, from the basic consideration of what to do with the dead body to the matter of coffins, cremation urns, gravestones, cemetery plots, *memento mori*, photographs of the deceased (especially popular in the late nineteenth century), mourning clothes, mourning jewelry, and more.[18] Floral wreaths and bouquets are typical offerings at Christian funerals; small rocks or pebbles are often left at Jewish gravesites; gifts of food and other items are expected during 'Day of the Dead' observances in Latino Catholic cultures; gifts to honor ancestors are typically brought to Japanese Shinto shrines. 'Dead man shirts,' memorial t-shirts that commemorate murder victims and feature photos of the deceased along with rap music lyrics, are popular today among young black mourners in New Orleans and elsewhere.[19] While these things constitute certain aspects of the commemoration of the dead, they do not entirely define it. The plethora of stuff accumulated at temporary memorials, on the other hand, almost over-determines the commemoration of grief.

In part, this has to do with how easy, and inexpensive, it is to participate in this materialist memorial culture. Corner grocery stores are often conveniently stocked with the typical, cheap stuff of temporary memorials: bouquets of flowers (real and artificial), small stuffed animals, balloons, votive candles, condolence cards, and more. Still, the sheer availability of these inexpensive items does not account for why the things that comprise these ephemeral memorials have become fundamental to contemporary expressions of public grief. Questions remain about why so much importance is attached to these material offerings, and how they have become ritualized and socially approved – indeed, even expected – in today's public performances of mourning.

Temporary memorials are the creative products of human thought and emotional need that help to mediate the psychic crisis of sudden and often inexplicable loss. The material culture of grief that they embody demonstrates the faith that contemporary audiences place in things to negotiate complex moments and events, such as traumatic death. Things work to satisfy the emotional needs of this negotiation: flowers, for example, symbolize the beauty and brevity of life, as do balloons. Hand-written notes, condolence cards, poems, and letters give voice to the grief-stricken and permit intimate conversations with (and confessions to) the deceased. Stuffed animals, and in particular teddy bears, intimate lost innocence. These things are central to contemporary public recollections of loss and social performances of grief not only because they are inexpensive and easily available but because they resonate with literalist beliefs in the symbolic and emotional power of material culture. Things, especially public things, map political cultures and shape political bodies; things, Bruno Latour argues, constitute 'atmospheres of democracy' and *dingpolitik* provides clearer and more credible possibilities than *realpolitik*.[20] Things also, of course, constitute a modern mass culture that valorizes impermanence and disposability in order to fuel patterns of consumption; as Arjun Appadurai argues, one of the hallmarks of modernity has been the organization of consumer desire around 'the aesthetics of ephemerality.' Still, however ephemeral the material culture of temporary memorials, significance can be found in how they work to mediate, permit, and encourage the social release of grief. However impermanent (at least initially), temporary memorials shoulder 'a great deal of social weight.'[21]

Like other forms of public commemoration, temporary memorials are memory aids. They specifically function to remember the recently, suddenly dead: to make their loss visible and public; to render their deaths memorable – never to be forgotten. Hand-written cards reading 'The World Will Never Forget You' were common among the spontaneous memorials erected to Princess Diana; likewise, many of the letters that appeared at the six major shrines built to Pim Fortuyn throughout the Netherlands included sentiments such as 'Dearest Pim, we will never forget you! In our hearts forever.'[22]

Temporary memorials flood the memories of their visitors; the mundane, familiar things of which they are made trigger personal associations. Their materialist dimensions mediate between the living and the dead as flowers, cards, photographs, and other objects 'have connotations of transience as well as permanence which feed into the metaphors used to describe and account for the capabilities of memory.' These things are meant to bind the living and the dead, and 'preserve a material presence in the face of an embodied absence.'[23] And because their ephemeral nature might sever this psychic bond, temporary memorials are increasingly being preserved.

Temporary memorials rarely feature precious materials, and being outdoors are generally subject to weeks of ruinous environmental conditions. Yet they are increasingly regarded as unique, valuable, and irreplaceable collections entitled to as much respect, preservation, and admiration as treasures uncovered at ancient temples. Most of the thousands of items affixed to Oklahoma City's Memory Fence, amassed at the Columbine High School memorial in 1999, and left at the temporary memorials erected to Fortuyn in Rotterdam, Amsterdam, and The Hague were saved. In Oklahoma City, they were collected, catalogued, and stored in a local warehouse maintained by a museum-trained archivist. In Colorado, they were archived within collections maintained by the Littleton Historical Museum and the Colorado Historical Society (Denver). In Amsterdam, they were preserved in the Pim Fortuyn Archive at the Meertens Institute.[24] Like the thousands of offerings left at the Vietnam Veterans Memorial in Washington, D.C., which are regularly culled by the United States National Park Service and preserved and catalogued in a suburban Maryland storage facility, the things left at temporary memorials are treated as things worth saving.[25] As staff at the Colorado Historical Society were advised during a 'Columbine Memorial Recovery Strategy Meeting':

We are working for the public and this event will be documented by the media...We will save everything. Everything will be collected and removed from the site. Later decisions will be made as to how the mementoes will be handled. There will be no dumpsters. We need to be sensitive. Members of the volunteer teams may have been directly affected by this event. Everything will be recovered.[26]

In May 1999, over a hundred volunteers spent three days collecting the offerings that were left at Columbine's memorial. Rotted flowers became compost for Denver area parks; fresher flowers became potpourri for victims' families. Everything else was archived.

Public institutions are increasingly being called upon to save and store temporary memorials. In December 2001, United States Senator Kit Bond, Representative Missouri, introduced a measure authorizing $5 million in federal funding for the Smithsonian National Museum of American History 'to collect and preserve items of historical significance' specific to 9/11, including six million tons of debris collected from the World Trade Center. 'It makes sense that since this was a national tragedy,' Bond remarked, 'our national historical repository get on top of it and organize it.'[27]

The attacks of September 11 certainly intensified this contemporary 'scramble to curate disaster,' as Bill Brown puts it. This is witnessed in both the plethora of objects and images that were generated and the vast numbers of exhibitions in which they were displayed: from 'The Day Our World Changed: Children's Art of 9/11' at the Museum of the City of New York in 2002, to 'Elegy in the Dust: Sept. 11th and the Chelsea Jeans Memorial' at the New York Historical Society in 2006. Yet if perhaps more visually dominant because of the enormous media and scholarly attention that has followed these objects, images, and exhibitions, the museal impulses surrounding 9/11 were hardly unique.[28] Following the Columbia Space Shuttle explosion in 2003, for example, staff at the Smithsonian National Air and Space Museum (Washington, D.C.) organized a temporary memorial in the museum's main hall, near a fifteen-foot tall model of the space shuttle.

Visitors brought bouquets of flowers, candles, cards, and a copy of the Torah, signed their names in the two public comment books that the museum provided, and posed for photos in front of the display. Collecting and displaying such space shuttle shrine material – called 'grief's memorabilia' by staffers – has now become part of the museum's curatorial agenda.[29]

Temporary memorial created in September 2001 featuring a teddy bear and flowers at the Pentagon, Arlington, VA. Photo Erika Doss.

Expectations that temporary memorials should be saved – or even made – by public museums and archives raise enormous practical and ethical questions, which museum professionals themselves struggle to answer. Can we realistically expect under-funded and overburdened public institutions to collect, process, house, and display the vast stuff of temporary memorials? Should museums be 'managing' these memorials, which means removing them from their visibly public environments (when? after how long?) and then storing them in sanitized and generally less accessible archives?[30] However these issues are considered, the fact remains that temporary memorials made of ephemeral and often base materials have assumed honorific status. Their prestige lies in perceptions of their embodiment of public emotions, and of a public culture of emotions being deemed eminently worthy of attention and preservation. More directly, temporary memorials are valued as the literal manifestation of public grief.

Public Grief

Grief is the most obviously employed affect in the making and meaning of temporary memorials. Grief is generally understood as the expression of deep emotional anguish, usually about death and loss, while mourning is defined as the ritualized practices that help assuage that anguish. Modern Western assumptions that grief is a private, internal emotion and that mourning is an external, social behavior are increasingly challenged today, as the widespread presence of temporary memorials alone suggests. In fact, these memorials problematize supposed distinctions between grief and mourning, as they embody both visibly public expressions of grief and performative rituals of mourning. They also embody contemporary understandings of continued, rather than severed, bonds between the living and the dead.

In 'Mourning and Melancholia' (1917), Freud argued that mourning was crucial in terms of 'working through' grief, indeed, that mourning was necessary in order for the grief-stricken to free themselves ('decathect') from psychologically dangerous attachments to the dead. 'When the work of mourning is completed,' said Freud, 'the ego becomes free and uninhibited again.' Those who failed to do this, who could not take measure of their loss and separate themselves from the deceased, were dysfunctionally subsumed by self-serving melancholia, which Freud regarded as a pathological form of grief, or melancholia.[31] This was a modernist approach to grief and mourning, prompted by assumptions about rationality and early twentieth-century urges toward order and efficiency. Grief was viewed as a disruptive and debilitating emotion, one that had to be dealt with – 'worked through' – as quickly as possible, hence the emphasis on severing ties with the dead, with 'letting go' and 'getting over it,' and moving on with one's life.

Although Freud's thesis stemmed from his own particular interests in ego development and Oedipal crises (the detachment of the child from the parent), not from the physical and emotional contexts of death and loss, this 'breaking bonds' presupposition became the cornerstone of modern Western psychoanalytic understandings of bereavement. It remains common in the rhetoric of grieving today: the huge temporary memorial that was created following the shootings at Columbine High School, for example, was repeatedly described in curative and healing terms, as part of a process of 'working through' and 'finding closure' for grief. The temporary memorials and Silent Marches that followed the Volendam café fire in 2001 played similarly instrumental coping roles. Yet Freud's own experiences with grief led him to recognize the limitations of his original theory and to subsequently revise and redefine his understandings of mourning.[32] More recent theoretical and clinical analyses of grief, which are based on how and why people actually grieve rather than on essentializing modernist interests in controlling their emotional responses to loss, contextualize grief within the particularities of lived experience, and emphasize the inseparability of life from death – or the 'continuing' bonds between the living and the deceased.

Some contemporary theorists argue, for example, that melancholia and bereavement are constant, if not central, in the formation of African American and/or homosexual identity. As José Esteban Muñoz writes: 'Melancholia, for blacks and queers of any color, is not a pathology but an integral part of everyday lives... a mechanism that helps us (re)construct identity and take our dead to the various battles we must wage in their names – and in our names.'[33] Mourning is particular to personal experience and injunctions against it, such authors argue, need to be recognized as injunctions against the personhood and subjectivity of the bereaved. Clinical researchers such as Dennis Klass and Phyllis Silverman similarly maintain that bereavement should be considered an unending cognitive and emotional process that 'affects the mourner for the rest of his or her life. People are changed by the experience; they do not get over it, and part of the change is a transformed but continuing relationship with the deceased.'[34] Mourning, in other words, is often endless although it need not be endlessly obsessive or pathological.

Recognition of grief's enduring presence has fostered great interest in the subject. A veritable 'grief industry' has developed, replete with best-selling books like *How to Go On Living When Someone You Love Dies* (1988), *Tuesdays with Morrie* (1997), and *Talking with Children About Loss* (1999). Online chatrooms and 'grief-share' websites (including griefnet.org, webhealing.com, and petloss.com) are also popular, providing comfort and support from volunteer traumatologists, extensive bibliographies on any number of 'grief-related topics,' and directions on how to create a virtual memorial. 'Grief and crisis management' policies scripted by mental health professionals specially trained in trauma and disaster response are being adopted in numerous public schools. If obviously attuned to today's cultural renegotiation of what grief means, the prescriptive tendencies of the grief industry are mostly pragmatic and highly opportunistic. Rather than recognizing causes, determining preventative measures, or considering the continuous and non-pathological dimensions of grief itself, many industry professionals see grief in terms of psychic pain and emotional damage, as a problematic 'stage' or phase that must be coped with and 'worked through' in order to return to normalcy.[35]

Armies of professional grief and trauma therapists are typically deployed by American schools today to 'address the emotional needs of students' and 'help them cope' with death and loss. Following the murder of six-year old Jon Benet Ramsay in 1996 in Boulder, Colorado, the elementary school that she had attended organized three days of grief counseling sessions for students. Following the shootings at Columbine High School, hundreds of grief industry professionals were dispatched to nearby churches and community centers by the Victims Services Unit of the Jefferson County Sheriff's Department, the Colorado Organization for Victim Assistance, and the Red Cross.

Schools throughout the Denver region organized public forums and candlelight vigils 'to assist parents and community members in managing their feelings and to offer information on how to help children cope with their feelings.' When Columbine's students returned to their high school a few weeks after the murders, a mental health counselor was present in every classroom to guide 'psychological debriefing.'[36] Following the attacks on the World Trade Center, several thousand grief and crisis counselors descended on New York, many of them trained in 'Critical-Incident Stress Management' (CISM, also called 'emotional first aid') and eager to ask questions like 'what was the worst part of the incident for you personally?'[37] Whether a high-profile media event like the shootings at Columbine or a more typical if no less heartbreaking daily tragedy such as the deaths of American teenagers in car accidents (7,460 in 2005), grief industry professionals are on the scene.

The benefits of extensive grief counseling are speculative, especially given growing recognition of the endless and non-pathological trajectory of bereavement and recent conclusions by researchers that 'generic interventions, targeted toward the general population of the bereaved, are likely to be unnecessary and largely unproductive.' As one grief industry professional herself remarks: 'There were far too many helpers at Columbine. Perhaps we need to look at our own egos and motivations. Do we all need to be at the front lines of a public tragedy?' Likewise, some question both the self-promotional tendencies of trauma therapy and the 'threat' it poses to individual self-reliance and national confidence.[38] Nevertheless, visibly public discussions and displays of grief are flourishing, as seen in both the popularity of bereavement counseling and the ubiquity of temporary memorials. Both are increasingly considered critical components in the management of grief.

The emotional life of public memorials is almost universally recognized in the form of roadside shrines. In the American southwest, wood and stone *descanos* were originally erected to memorialize those who died suddenly, did not receive last rites, and were buried in unconsecrated ground, in hopes that travelers along the same roads might stop and say prayers for the souls of the deceased. Eighteenth-century territorial governors and bishops tried to ban these roadside memorials, worried that they might scare off new settlers or that the practice constituted a threat to prescribed political and/or religious authority.[39] Yet they continued to be erected and, especially in the twentieth century, increased along with the growth of highways and car culture. In 2004, 42,836 Americans died in traffic accidents, compared with 804 in the Netherlands, 4,741 in Spain, and 8,492 in Japan. There is no specific national monument to these deaths – because, as Michael Warner observes, it is *mass* disaster that commands national subjectivity.[40] But there are thousands of local roadside memorials, usually erected by family members and friends seeking solace in their grief. Such memorials are visibly public modes of mourning which aim to manage, to order and control, the psychic disaster of death and loss.

Their heightened public presence is commanding increased popular and critical attention: recent films on roadside memorials include the suspense thriller *Descanos* (2006) and the documentary *Resting Places* (2007), and recent songs include Don Morrell's folkie ballad 'Roadside Cross' (1999). Roadside memorials have been examined in detail at academic conferences, in numerous scholarly articles, and on a burgeoning number of websites. One internet entrepreneur even sells 'Road Side Memorial Crosses' in redwood or oak, tipped with gold corners, and accompanied by a floral arrangement and a protective picture cover containing a photo of the deceased.[41] Their abundance, and some argue, agency – in that some view roadside memorials as 'expressions of alternative authority drawn from the intensity of grief [and] from a belief in the spiritual presence of the deceased' – is also increasingly subject to state and legal scrutiny.[42] In America, for example, many states have enacted legislation banning or restricting temporary roadside memorials for reasons of highway safety (arguing that they are driving distractions) and for issues related to separation of church and state. Other states have opted to allow only officially approved roadside memorials: plaques and markers, usually installed for limited periods (such as one to six years), that serve as cautionary signs about driving while intoxicated, or as reminders to watch for pedestrians and bicyclists.[43]

Various county councils have pursued similar bans in England. In 2003, on the anniversary of Princess Diana's death, RoadPeace, a UK charity for victims of traffic accidents, launched its 'Remember Me' roadside memorial campaign: a series of signs, each featuring a red flower (a scarlet anemone, a flower associated in mythology with love and loss) dripping three drops of blood onto the words 'Remember Me.' In just a few years, hundreds of the signs had been erected at the sites of fatal crash scenes throughout the country.[44]

Temporary memorials and roadside shrines are intrinsically *public* memorials. If modern Western social and cultural conventions insisted on private and individual forms of grieving throughout much of the twentieth century, viewing the bereaved as psychologically disabled and hence social pariahs, contemporary mourning practices are visibly public and participatory. Changing understandings of the enduring trajectory of grief and the performative and experiential nature of mourning, as well as repetitious media attention to the felt experiences of traumatic death and loss, have helped make grief an increasingly permissible public emotion. Likewise, revisionist understandings of trauma discourse and collective bereavement within particular communities have significantly altered how grief is negotiated. As a result, localized losses are often claimed today on broader public, and national, terms. 'What happened in Littleton pierced the soul of America,' President Bill Clinton proclaimed one year after the shootings at Columbine High School. Likewise, as Ed Linenthal remarked in 1998, the grassroots grieving displayed on Memory Fence intimated 'that the deaths in Oklahoma have become, like the deaths in the Holocaust, public deaths that count not only for the families but the nation.'[45] Yet because they are visibly public in the national imaginary, contemporary modes of mourning such as temporary memorials and roadside shrines are also framed by particular measures, or codes, of control.

Items being added to the Memory Fence, Oklahoma City, OK, in 1999.
Photo Erika Doss.

Mourning Codes

The period immediately following traumatic death, or death in general, is typically viewed in any number of cultures as psychologically uncertain and hence socially and politically dangerous. 'The passion of grief is volatile,' remarks Gail Holst-Warhaft, and mourning rituals are devised to wrest order out of disorder, to provide structure and give meaning to the ineffable, and to prevent psychic and social anarchy.[46] From the moment of eruptive trauma to the final collection of their wilted flowers, ruined cards, and soggy teddy bears, temporary memorials are manufactured according to particular cultural codes which include siting the memorial directly at or as close as possible to the locus of death; making offerings of culturally symbolic importance such as flowers, photos, condolence cards, and stuffed animals; openly demonstrating emotional behaviors such as sobbing and hugging; and directly eliciting references to religious intervention. These codes are socially reinforced through mass media coverage: as Mervi Pantti argues, for example, newspapers and talk shows played a large role in manufacturing the public display of grief following the murder of Ana Lindh, the Foreign Minister of Sweden, in 2003.[47] And they are further advanced by expanded understandings of permissible public emotions.

To some degree, mourning codes are instituted in order to objectify and depersonalize grief, thereby assuring 'that the psychic crisis engendered by loss, especially in its initial stages, will not plunge the mourner into sheer delirium or catalepsy.'[48] Socially shared and culturally familiar, these codes shift localized traumas – the plane crash in Eindhoven, the bombing in Oklahoma, the attacks on the World Trade Center – into nationally mediated 'events,' and also curtail the threat that violent death and disaster might pose to the collective psyche and national order.[49] Temporary memorials, and the various commemorative cultures that appropriate their affective conventions, thereby orchestrate consensual understandings of tragic death's purpose and meaning. Indeed, as a social affect conditioned by what Alistair Thomson terms 'popular memory,' the public mourning embodied in temporary memorials 'demonstrates the ways in which expressions of grief, far from being 'outside' politics, are always framed within dominant narrative forms and genres.'[50]

Consider, for example, the manner in which mourning was managed by the *New York Times* in its nationally syndicated 'Portraits of Grief' column, which appeared in the newspaper three days after 9/11 and continued until late December 2001. Initially called 'Among the Missing,' the *Times*'s series originated in the handmade missing-person flyers that circulated immediately after 9/11, which featured detailed personal details and photographs, were taped onto every available public surface near ground zero, and then – as these missing became the dead – formed the basis for countless temporary memorials. Ephemeral, impressionistic, and ritualistic, much like the memorials on which they were clearly modeled, the newspaper's 'Portraits of Grief' were snapshots of affect: 200-word profiles, usually accompanied by tiny head-shots, which casually sketched the preferred pastimes (parties, dancing, golf, fly-fishing) and endearing qualities (loved to laugh, loved to cook) of the victims of 9/11. Intimate and anecdotal, these sketches were the seeming antithesis to the cold eulogies of the typical newspaper obituary – much as temporary memorials may be seen as the emotional opposites of permanent granite monuments.

Yet 'Portraits of Grief' were also informed by formulaic codes of bereavement, or what David Simpson likens as the 'Taylorization of mourning.' Few of the *Times* portraits included the details of death, and most emphasized cheerful and upbeat moments in the lives of the dead. Assuming that the victims of the attacks of 9/11 were an essentially heteronormative group (few of the newspaper portraits alluded to sexual difference), the *Times* sketches 'were almost all versions of the same story – happy people, fulfilled in their jobs, fountains of love and charity, pillars of their family and community... a flourishing civil society indifferent to race, gender, and economic category.'[51] The potentially disordering grief of 9/11 was thereby managed as a national ordeal that was experienced, and endured, by everyone. More critically engaged questions of why and how 9/11 happened, and to whom, were sidestepped in deference to a consensual national discourse that ultimately paved the way for the war on terror.

Death Matters

Memory 'is rarely conceived as a cemetery,' writes William Gass.[52] Yet temporary memorials are almost always memorials to the dead, and as such are best understood in terms of highly conflicted modern attitudes about death. For most of the twentieth century, the United States was characterized as a death-denying society in which public discussions of dying, death, and bereavement were essentially taboo, and death itself largely relegated to the institutional and private settings of the hospital. Sixty percent of Americans, for example, die in hospitals, and an additional sixteen percent die in nursing homes or hospices.[53] Contemporary debates about abortion, euthanasia, gun control, living wills, organ transplantation, and stem cell research, as well as popular interests in 'good death,' the afterlife, and bereavement therapies, suggest heightened attention to issues of death and dying. Growing trends toward funeral preplanning, and the global

jackets, concert posters, sneakers, sports equipment, and Bibles left at Columbine High School's temporary memorial summoned the taste and faith cultures of the school's slain students (and one teacher). The flowers, t-shirts, teddy bears, and religious ephemera that made up the memorial created in April 2007 at Virginia Tech University (Blacksburg, Virginia), where a school shooting left thirty-two students and faculty dead, evoked the personalities and spiritual beliefs of those who died. The floral tributes, bottles of wine, cigars, and dog figurines left at the temporary memorials to Pim Fortuyn were tributes related to his lifestyle and personality (he owned two dogs, for example). Such memorials are also, of course, often awash in the mementos of sorrow and affection most personally meaningful to their mourners, hence the occasionally odd juxtaposition of 'contradictory objects such as crosses and teddy bears, bibles, and beer cans.'[60]

While temporary memorials commemorate traumatic and sudden death, and speak to loss and absence, the dead themselves remain very much alive: visibly present in the photographs, clothes, and possessions left by mourners; 'persistently social' in the cards and poems addressed to them.[61] This might suggest the denial of death, or the inability to acknowledge human finality and reckon with loss, at least in the time period immediately following sudden and traumatic death. It also suggests a primary motivation in the making of temporary memorials, which is to commemorate grief. Obviously, all memorials commemorate presentist interests and ambitions; the dead, after all, are dead. But the materialist, kinesthetic, and emotional dimensions of temporary memorials *are* their raison d'etre, and much of their meaning lies in their own public performances of bereavement. As Peter Jan Margry and Christina Sánchez-Carretero argue: 'Improvised memorials should be read as more than an expression of grief. They are performative events in public spaces.'[62]

Their meaning further lies in the symbolic authority of those being grieved – the dead. Over the past fifty years, the United States – like other nations – has 'invested heavily' in managing and controlling death:

Roadside memorial erected in 2003, Austin, TX. Photo Erika Doss.

We have eradicated many previously fatal diseases and control others with medical technology. Infant mortality rates have plunged while adult life expectancy has surged. We have developed automobile air bags, emergency response systems, warning devices, and safety standards for nearly everything that could put our lives at risk. Even our risk of dying in war has been reduced by strategies such as airstrikes rather than deployment of ground troops. We have gained such control over death that we now expect to die only of old age.'[63]

In 2005, the Center for Disease Control announced that average life expectancy for Americans reached 77.6 years (80.1 for women; 74.8 years for men). This is low by comparison with other countries: in the Netherlands, for example, according to United Nations statistics compiled in 2006, life expectancy is 81.9 years for women and 77.5 for men; in Sweden it is 83.0 for women and 78.7 for men; in Japan it is 86.1 for women and 79.0 for men.

Thus, when sudden, violent, senseless, and traumatic death does occur, especially in 'safe' settings such as public schools and federal office buildings, and especially among young people, shock occurs. Temporary memorials convey this shock and simultaneously organize social and cultural understandings of the dead. As Robert Pogue Harrison remarks, 'obligation to the corpse' is among the more revealing of social indices, and Western culture has long operated under the assumption that human remains demand appropriate ceremonial rites of burial and prayer in order for the psychic release and alleviation of grief. Recovery and ritual observance of the dead is crucial, argues Zoë Crossland, in order to properly situate them within the realms of individual and collective memory, and thereby 'remake' the world of the living.[64] Bodies that are not properly mourned and buried become spectres: haunting and restless reminders of life out of order.

This helps to explain the dramatic and dangerous recovery efforts undertaken after the attacks on New York's World Trade Center on September 11, 2001, in which rescue personnel focused on finding the dead – after it was determined that there would be few survivors – at great detriment to their own health and welfare. Record numbers of firefighters deployed to the Twin Towers developed serious respiratory ailments and symptoms of post-traumatic stress disorder.[65] For ten months after 9/11, local authorities in New York sifted through millions of tons of debris searching for human remains, eventually recovering some 19,000 fragments. Millions of dollars were spent trying to match them to the names of the missing, and while 1,594 of the 2,749 people who died in the World Trade Center were identified, thousands of human fragments remain unidentified. In 2005, members of 'WTC Families for a Proper Burial' filed a federal lawsuit against the City of New York, demanding that Staten Island's Fresh Kills landfill, a now-closed 2,200-acre site where most of the debris from the World Trade Center was deposited, be re-opened for further recovery and removal operations. City plans to convert the site into a huge public park (three times the size of Central Park) and 9/11 memorial were contested by grieving families suing over the right to recover and properly bury their dead. 'Our loved ones need to be put in a final resting place with dignity,' one woman remarked. 'Our family will not stop fighting this until we have a proper burial place.' During construction and rebuilding at the World Trade Center site, hundreds of human remains, mostly bone fragments, were recovered.[66]

Desires to possess the dead also explain the demands of the bereaved following other tragedies: such as when EgyptAir Flight 990 crashed into the waters off Nantucket in October 1999, and grieving relatives insisted on the immediate retrieval of bodies, although debris had sunk in nearly 300 feet of water, a storm generated twenty-two-foot waves, and the entire area was described by the Navy's senior salvage expert as 'pitch black.'[67] And they explain how the USS *Arizona* became a national memorial in Pearl Harbor, Hawaii. Since the Civil War, the United States has made the recovery, identification, return, and proper burial of military fatalities a national priority. Despite military protocol and public expectations, however, most of the bodies (over 1,000) inside the USS *Arizona*, struck by Japanese bombers on December 7, 1941, were simply unrecoverable. The shock of the sudden attack made the slogan 'Remember Pearl Harbor' the rallying cry of World War II; the battleship interment of its soldier dead legitimated the dedication of the USS *Arizona* as sacred ground, as a war grave and national memorial, in 1962.[68]

Dead bodies, Katherine Verdery explains, have enormous symbolic power: 'They evoke the awe, uncertainty, and fear associated with "cosmic" concerns, such as the meaning of life and death.' Dead bodies have sacred, obligatory connotations but are also malleable and ambiguous. As such, they are particularly efficacious political symbols which play central roles in shaping and reshaping national identities and narratives. Today's recovery of the victims of the Spanish Civil War, of the prisoners of the Soviet gulag, of those slaughtered in German death camps, Cambodian killing fields, and Rwandan forests is similarly oriented to the remaking of national history and memory in those places. As Verdery remarks, 'dead bodies animate the study of politics.'[69] They certainly play central performative and political roles in contemporary commemorative cultures: most temporary memorials, for example, are erected at, or near, the sites where tragic and traumatic death occurred. Their construction, and the public display of grief that they embody, largely depends on contemporary, and widely shared, understandings of memory and history.

Memory and Public Feeling

'Welcome to the memory industry,' bids Kerwin Klein in a discussion of the swell of 'memory studies' in academic scholarship and the influence of theorists such as Maurice Halbwachs and historians such as Pierre Nora. The study of memory – the word comes from the Latin *memor*, meaning mindful – is itself fairly recent, originating in late nineteenth-century cognitive psychology and understood by Freud, for example, as the private agent of unconscious mental processes, as a tool which individuals could use to retrieve information from the past. Today, the study of memory 'extends considerably beyond psychology,' writes Barbie Zelizer, and is a salient feature of academic discourse in disciplines ranging from anthropology and mass communication to cultural geography, literary criticism, and art history. Likewise, incipient concepts of memory's essentially privatizing agency have shifted to considerations of its performativity and, especially, to how acts of remembering are key to the formation, and reformation, of social identity. As Jay Winter remarks, today's 'memory boom' is directly related to today's identity politics: to the emergence of multiple social and political groups claiming voice and vying for representation in the public sphere. [70] Memory's original meaning as a mindful presence in and toward the world has considerably expanded to the legitimization of that presence on copious terms.

The past few decades have seen a burgeoning of theoretical, social, and cultural projects centered on memory, ranging from the publication of Nora's multi-volume anthology *Les Lieux de Mémoire* (1984-1992) to the heated psychotherapeutic and legal debates surrounding issues of repressed and recovered memory. [71] Memory work today includes flourishing popular interests in autobiography, memoirs, and family genealogy, and growing public commemorations of the Holocaust in memorials, museums, and rituals of remembrance, such as ceremonies held in 2005 recalling the sixtieth anniversary of the liberation of Auschwitz-Birkenau by Soviet troops on January 27, 1945. Memory today is defined in terms of all sorts of cultural practices, material artifacts, and national narratives, from family reunions and

Temporary memorial created in April 2007 at Virginia Tech University, Blacksburg, VA. Photo Erika Doss.

scrapbook photographs to annual civic celebrations such as Cinco de Mayo and July 4th in the United States to Remembrance of the Dead in the Netherlands, an annual commemoration (on May 4) of Dutch losses in warfare.

Understood as collective social ritual, redemptive agent, subaltern expression, and/or mode of identity politics, memory's montage of meanings dominate contemporary cultural sensibilities. Memory evades timeless categories, which helps to account for its broad appeal in a cultural climate where category challenging is the norm. Among other clichés, memory is valorized for refusing to 'stand still': for being elusive and unstable, open-ended and unresolved. It is further embraced as an active agent which is performative and experiential: personal, presentist, fleeting. Yet its contemporary dominance may especially relate to its material and visual presence; as Nora remarks, memory 'relies on the materiality of the trace, the immediacy of the recording, the visibility of the image.' Or as Juliet Mitchell explains: 'Memory comes into being only after the trace which marks it: there is no thing, no event, experience, feeling, to remember, there is only that present which an empty past brings into being.'[72]

Indeed, much as the memorial has supplanted the monument, memory has superceded contemporary understandings of history. Memory's popular and academic appeal, Klein and others observe, has a lot to do with contemporary perceptions of history's repugnance: 'Our sudden fascination with memory goes hand in hand with postmodern reckonings of history as the marching black boot and of historical consciousness as an oppressive fiction. Memory can come to the fore in an age of historiographic crisis precisely because it figures as a therapeutic alternative to historical discourse.'[73] Following this binary, history is condemned as hard cold facts and monolithic master narratives, while memory is welcomed as the emotional and intimate feelings of 'real people,' especially those formerly excluded from grand historical projects. History is demonized as the remote and dusty past; memory extolled as its immediate, intimate, and presentist alternative. Memory, Nora contends, is 'affective and magical' while history, 'because it is an intellectual and secular production' is consigned to 'analysis and criticism.' History, he adds, 'is perpetually suspicious of memory, and its true mission is to suppress and destroy it.' History is memory's enemy, bent on 'deforming and transforming it, penetrating and petrifying it.'[74]

Obviously, these sorts of distinctions are reductive and untenable: memory and history can both be careless and capricious; neither is necessarily more authentic than the other. Memory is the 'bedrock' of history, Paul Ricoeur wrote, arguing for reconsiderations of their reciprocity and reconciliation.[75] Indeed, contemporary notions of memory and history are largely indistinct because knowledge and identity are increasingly acquired and understood on experiential and affective terms. Historians Roy Rosenzweig and David Thelen, for example, found strong connections regarding the 'presence of the past' when they interviewed several thousand Americans in the mid-1990s for a study of popular history.[76] In forms ranging from high school reunions to heritage tourism, the history that is most meaningful to Americans today is personal and participatory, and especially keyed to individual and familial memories. For many Americans of color, 'history' means shared experiences particular to race and ethnicity,

Temporary memorial (photo taken in 2005) created in memory of United Flight 93 and 9/11, Shanksville, PA. Photo Erika Doss.

including tribal and community traditions, the struggles of slavery and civil rights, and the recollected experiences of incarceration on federal reservations or in World War II internment camps.

Today's 'memory boom' reflects less, then, a declension of historical consciousness than a cultural shift toward public feeling, toward affective modes of knowledge and comprehension. Indeed, today's memorial mania is simultaneous with an 'experiential turn' in contemporary understandings of history, memory, and identity.[77] Consider the popularity of interactive museum exhibitions, where audiences emulate historical actors and actions. At the U.S. Holocaust Memorial Museum in Washington, D.C., for example, visitors are given identity cards of Holocaust victims and walk through a Nazi-era freight car. At the Sixth Floor Museum in Dallas, visitors stand near the 'Sniper's Nest' in the building's southeast corner, where Lee Harvey Oswald fired the shots that killed President John F. Kennedyin 1963. (A live 'Earthcam' feed from the site has generated millions of hits.) At the National Civil Rights Museum in Memphis, visitors walk into the rooming house bathroom where James Earl Ray fired the shots that killed Dr. Martin Luther King, Jr. Across the street, they can peek inside the motel room where King died – and where his unmade bed and dishes from his last meal, along with cigarette-filled ashtrays and a copy of the April 4, 1968 *Memphis Press-Scimitar*, are all on public display. As the museum's website notes: 'The emotional focus of the museum and the historical climax of the exhibit is the Lorraine Motel, where Dr. King was assassinated. Dr. King's room can be viewed as it was on April 4, 1968.'[78] At night, an acid-green laser beam follows the trajectory of Ray's bullet from the rooming house bathroom to the balcony of the motel where King was shot.

Alison Landsberg maintains that new forms of public cultural memory and mass technology – what she calls 'prosthetic memory' – enable anyone to personally experience the past, no matter how remote or distant.[79] Most importantly, the desire to do so stems from the increasingly affective dimensions of contemporary culture. Today, visceral modes of experience are regarded as the primary vehicles of knowledge and identity acquisition. Of course, as Joan Scott argues, discourses of experience are both illuminating and highly problematic: they give visibility to often marginalized historical subjects but also buffer them from critique when 'experience' is understood as authentic, or is essentially reproduced as an epistemology of fact. The key, says Scott, is to 'attend to the historical processes that, through discourse, position subjects and produce their experiences. It is not individuals who have experience, but subjects who are constituted through experience.'[80] The critical project is to examine how practices of remembering – and forgetting – are central to the construction of private, public, individual, and collective identities.

The emotional life of public memorials is especially dependent on the fact that temporary memorials are created to be experienced: to be felt, not simply to be seen. As Carole Blair observes, memorials exert 'obvious work on the body' by directing 'the vector, speed, or possibilities of physical movement.'[81] This is especially true of temporary memorials. Usually erected at unexpected sites of unanticipated tragedy, such memorials are often aggressively physical entities: spaces that must be walked around and through (literally, if they block a sidewalk or occupy vast acres in a park); places that demand our physical interaction. Temporary memorials, like most memorials, are destina-

A sea of flowers, objects and documents in front of Pim Fortuyn's residence, May 2002.

tions: places and spaces to be visited. Fixed commemorative sites such as the Lincoln Memorial (Washington, D.C.) and the National Monument on the Dam (Amsterdam) are mostly sites to visit and look at, although they may also host annual rites of remembrance and other public ceremonies. Temporary memorials, however, originate as performative gestures of audience engagement. People bring things to temporary memorials, not only making them but also orchestrating their affective conditions. They walk through and around them; they read the cards and poems that are left; they kneel down to caress the other things that have been brought; they photograph and videotape what they see; they cry; they are physically and emotionally moved – affected – on multiple levels.

A kinesthetic paradigm has long informed Western commemorative culture: consider the performative rituals of circumambulation in ancient Greek funerals, or in honorific ceremonies conducted around Trajan's Column in imperial Rome. Consider the Christian practices of touching the crucifix at the altar, stroking the hem of a clothed statue of the Virgin, or kissing the revered icon of a saint. Consider how visitors touch the names of the dead inscribed on the Vietnam

Veterans Memorial in Washington, D.C., and make rubbings of those names on pieces of paper. Consider the compulsive obligation to frame and capture memorial culture on camera, and how such acts of visual documentation – the funeral of Princess Di is one prime example – have become the social norm. (Indeed, if photos of the dead were not uncommon a century ago, photos and videos of *mourners* of the dead are typical today.) All of these physical, intimate, and performative gestures shape the sustained meaning of temporary memorials. As C. Nadia Serematakis maintains, memory 'is a culturally mediated material practice that is activated by embodied acts and semantically dense objects.'[82] In contemporary cultures where experiential nuances have heightened significance, where knowledge and understanding are equated with felt experience – with being there and touching something, with 'feeling' the pain and suffering of others – temporary memorials are especially meaningful because of their essentially kinesthetic dimensions.

Conclusion

Grief is an intense and explosive emotion, a passion easily translated into violence and outrage. Temporary memorials embody this structure of feeling as well as efforts to assuage it: they both express and manage the psychic crisis and social disorder of death and loss via materialist and performative modes of mourning. Their burgeoning contemporary presence at sites of sudden death and places of traumatic loss, in memory of roadside fatalities, airplane crashes, political assassinations, victims of school shootings, victims of terrorism, and more, reveals both a cultural renegotiation of grief and the changed dimensions of mourning. While the subjects mourned in these memorials and those who perform these mourning practices are valued, it is the emotional life of contemporary public memorials that is deemed most memorable.

Not surprisingly, their obsessive materialism, emotional intensity, and widespread national popularity have triggered no small amount of 'hostile commentary' among journalists and academics alike. Some have criticized temporary memorials and spontaneous shrines for being 'too much' for the public sphere, with their overwrought displays seemingly straining the boundaries between good taste and vulgarity. In 2004, the conservative British think-tank Civitas mocked temporary memorials and the public display of grief as 'conspicuous compassion' and 'mourning sickness.'[83] More perceptive critics have tackled the problematic dimensions, in some cases, of what and who is being commemorated. In Australia, roadside memorials dedicated to young men killed in car accidents are persuasively explained by some cultural geographers as 'conservative memorials of youth machismo [and] heroic aggression' that serve to glorify 'dominant and problematic strains of masculinity.' Likewise, as I have written elsewhere, the spontaneous shrine erected at Columbine High School in 1999 served in large part to proselytize on behalf of evangelical Christianity, and to ignore the issues of teen alienation and gun violence that orchestrated its machination.[84] It is important to recognize that temporary memorials, and the contemporary cultures of public feeling that they embody, do not always yield the results that their analysts and critics may prefer – such as a cultural economy of radical social protest, or ritualized performances of civic affirmation and solidarity. Understanding them on critically nuanced terms calls for an emotional epistemology attuned to their historical context, social meaning, and political machination, and situated in their affective conditions and meanings.

Notes

*   This text is a revised version of a lecture given at the Meertens Instituut on March 30, 2006. My thanks to the audience for their questions and comments, and to David Morgan and Peter Jan Margry for their helpful criticism.

1.   Leslie George Katz, *The American Monument* (New York: The Eakins Press Foundation, 1976) n.p.

2.   For discussion of social response to contemporary disasters in the Netherlands see, in particular, Paul Post, Ronald L. Grimes, Albertina Nugteren, Per Pettersson, and Hessel Zondag, *Disaster Ritual: Explorations of an Emerging Ritual Repertoire* (Leuven, Belgium: Peeters Publishers, 2003).

3.   Erika Doss, *Memorial Mania: Self, Nation, and the Culture of Commemoration in Contemporary America* (forthcoming).

4.   For an overview of terminology, see Peter Jan Margry and Christina Sánchez-Carretero, 'Memorializing Traumatic Death,' *Anthropology Today* 23, no. 3 (June 2007) 1-2.

5.   Peter Jan Margry, 'Performative Memorials: Arenas on Political Resentment in Dutch Society,' in Peter Jan Margry and Herman Roodenburg, eds., *Reframing Dutch Culture: Between Otherness and Authenticity* (Aldershot: Ashgate, 2007), 109-133.

6.   This is similarly argued in *Disaster Ritual* (2003), a study of contemporary ritual dynamics in Dutch and international contexts, whose authors observe that the memorials, marches, and services that follow many disasters are 'strikingly coherent and orderly,' see p. 246.

7.   See, for example: Bob Bednar, 'Touching Images: Towards a Visual/Material Cultural Study of Roadside Shrines,' *Brown Working Papers in the Arts & Sciences*, Southwestern University 7 (2007), available at http:www/southwestern/edu/academic/bwp/vol7/bednar-vol7.pdf; Erika Doss, 'Death, Art, and Memory in the Public Sphere: The Visual and Material Culture of Grief in Contemporary America,' *Mortality* 7, no. 1 (2002), 63-82; Sylvia Grider, 'Public Grief and the Politics of Memorial,' *Anthropology Today* 23, no. 3 (June 2007), 3-7; C. Allen Haney, Christina Leimar, and Juliann Lowery, 'Spontaneous Memorialization: Violent Death and Emerging Mourning Ritual,' *Omega* 35, no. 2 (1997), 159-171; Cheryl R. Jorgensen-Earp and Lori A. Lanzilotti, 'Public Memory and Private Grief: The Construction of Shrines at Sites of Public Tragedy,' *Quarterly Journal of Speech* 84 (1998), 150-170; Peter Jan

Margry, 'The Murder of Pim Fortuyn and Collective Emotions: Hype, Hysteria, and Holiness in The Netherlands?' *Etnofoor: Antropologisch Tijdschrift* 16, no. 2 (2003), 106-131; and Irene Stengs, 'Ephemeral Memorials Against "Senseless Violence": Materialisations of Public Outcry' in *Etnofoor: Antropologisch Tijdschrift* 16, no. 2 (2003) 26-40.

8. Jack Santino, 'Not An Unimportant Failure: Rituals of Death and Politics in Northern Ireland,': *Displayed in Mortal Light*, ed. Michael McCaughan (Antrim, Northern Ireland: Antrim Arts Council, 1992), np.

9. Jack Santino, 'Performative Commemoratives: Spontaneous Shrines and the Public Memorialization of Death,' in *Spontaneous Shrines and the Public Memorialization of Death*, ed. Jack Santino (New York: Palgrave MacMillan, 2006), 13. See also Margry, 'Performative Memorials.'

10. Harriet F. Senie, 'Mourning in Protest: Spontaneous Memorials and the Sacralization of Public Space,' in *Spontaneous Shrines and the Public Memorialization of Death*, ed. Jack Santino (New York: Palgrave MacMillan, 2006), 45.

11. Jack Santino, *Signs of War and Peace: Social Conflict and the Use of Public Symbols in Northern Ireland* (New York: Palgrave, 2001), 103; Susanne Greenhalgh, 'Our Lady of Flowers: The Ambiguous Politics of Diana's Floral Revolution,' in *Mourning Diana: Nation, Culture, and the Performance of Grief* (London and New York: Routledge, 1999), 40-59; and George Monger and Jennifer Chandler, 'Pilgrimage to Kensington Palace,' *Folklore* 109 (1998), 104-108. For other discussions see *Planet Diana: Cultural Studies and Global Mourning*, ed. Ien Ang (Kingswood, NSW: Research Centre in Intercommunal Studies, University of Western Sydney, 1997), and *The Mourning for Diana*, ed. Tony Walter (London: Berg, 1999). On the other hand, surveys conducted shortly after Diana's death, asking informants to record their 'reflections, feelings, opinions, [and] observations' about her hyper-mediated demise, found diverse, ambiguous, and contradictory responses which counter notions that Diana's death was collectively, consensually, or critically mourned. See the detailed analysis compiled by James Thomas in *Diana's Mourning: A People's History* (Cardiff: University of Wales Press, 2002).

12. See, for example, *Roadside Memorials: A Multidisciplinary Approach*, ed. Jennifer Clark (Armidale, NSW: EMU Press, 2007); Holly Everett, *Roadside Crosses in Contemporary Memorial Culture* (Denton, TX: University of North Texas Press, 2002); George Monger, 'Modern Wayside Shrines,' *Folklore* 108 (1997), 113-114; and John Wolffe, 'Royalty

and Public Grief in Britain: An Historical Perspective 1819-1997,' in *The Mourning for Diana*, pp. 53-64.

13.   Ann Cvetkovich, *An Archive of Feelings: Trauma, Sexuality, and Lesbian Public Cultures* (Durham, NC: Duke University Press, 2003), 7.

14.   Regina Bendix, 'Introduction: Ear to Ear, Nose to Nose, Skin to Skin: 'The Senses in Comparative Ethnographic Perspective,' *Etnofoor* 18, no. 1 (2005), 1; Lauren Berlant, 'Critical Inquiry, Affirmative Culture,' *Critical Inquiry* 30 (Winter 2004), 446.

15.   Jules Prown, *Art as Evidence: Writings on Art and Material Culture* (New Haven: Yale University Press, 2002); Daniel Miller, ed., *Material Cultures: Why Some Things Matter* (Chicago: University of Chicago Press, 1998), 6.

16.   Pierre Nora, 'Between Memory and History,' *Representations* 26 (Spring 1989), 13.

17.   Doss, 'Death, Art, and Memory in the Public Sphere,' 66-67; Edward T. Linenthal, *The Unfinished Bombing: Oklahoma City in American Memory* (New York: Oxford University Press, 2001), 165-69, Kristin Hass suggests that as many as 'a million objects were carried to (and stuffed into)' Memory Fence in the first year after the bombing; see Kristin Ann Hass, *Carried to the Wall: American Memory and the Vietnam Veterans Memorial* (Berkeley: University of California Press, 1998) 126; Jane Thomas, curator of the Oklahoma City Memorial Foundation, says that this archive contains a collection of around 300,000 items; see Linenthal, *The Unfinished Bombing*, 167, 282-83, n. 77.

18.   Elizabeth Hallam and Jenny Hockey, *Death, Memory and Material Culture* (New York: Berg, 2001), 129-154 and passim; Jay Ruby, *Secure the Shadow: Death and Photography in America* (Cambridge, MA: MIT Press, 1995).

19.   Emily Yellin, 'New Orleans Epitaph: Dead Man Shirts,' *New York Times* (17 April 2000), A-15.

20.   Bruno Latour, 'Introduction: From *Realpolitik* to *Dingpolitik* or How to Make Things Public,' *Making Things Public: Atmospheres of Democracy*, eds. Bruno Latour and Peter Weibel (Cambridge: MIT Press, 2005), 16 and passim.

21.   Arjun Appadurai, *Modernity at Large: Cultural Dimensions of Globalization* (Minneapolis: University of Minnesota Press, 1996), 84; Rudi Colloredo-Mansfeld, 'Matter Unbound,' *The Journal of Material Culture* 8, no. 3 (November 2003), 252.

22.   Monger and Chandler, 'Pilgrimage to Kensington Palace,' 107; Margry, 'The Murder of Pim Fortuyn and Collective Emotions,' 117.

23. Hallam and Hockey, *Death, Memory and Material Culture*, 8.
24. On materials related to Fortuyn see Margry, 'The Murder of Pim Fortuyn and Collective Emotions,' n. 26, p. 128 and http://www.meertens. knaw.nl/meertensnet/wdb.php?sel=138759
25. By 1993, some 250,000 objects collected at the Vietnam Veterans Memorial had been collected and catalogued; see Hass, *Carried to the Wall* and Thomas Allen, *Offerings at the Wall: Artifacts from the Vietnam Veterans Memorial Collection* (Atlanta: Turner Publishing, 1995). On Oklahoma City's collection see Carol Brown, '"Out of the Rubble": Building a Contemporary History Archive – The Oklahoma City National Memorial Archives,' *Perspectives* (October 1999) at: http://www.historians.org/Perspectives/issues/1999/9910/9910EIP.CFM; accessed September 8, 2006.
26. Colorado Historical Society, 'Columbine Memorial Recovery Strategy Meeting, 6 May 1999,' memo, Decorative and Fine Arts Division, Colorado Historical Society, Denver, File Copy, Box 2000.130. By contrast, materials left on private grounds, such as Elvis's gravesite at Graceland, are generally not saved; see Erika Doss, *Elvis Culture: Fans, Faith, and Image* (Lawrence, KS: The University Press of Kansas, 1999), 102-104.
27. Bond quoted in Tara Burghart, 'Sept. 11 Artifacts in Demand,' *The Denver Post* (December 13, 2001) A-22.
28. Bill Brown, 'Commodity, Nationalism, and the Lost Object,' keynote lecture for 'The Pathos of Authenticity: American Passions of the Real,' John F. Kennedy-Institut für Nordamerikastudien, Berlin, June 21, 2007; on media and scholarly attention to 9/11's various cultural forms see, for example, *The Selling of 9/11: How a National Tragedy Became a Commodity*, ed. Dana Heller (New York: Palgrave, 2005), and Marita Sturken, *Tourists of History: Memory, Kitsch, and Consumerisn from Oklahoma City to Ground Zero* (Durham, NC: Duke University Press, 2007).
29. Valerie Neal, 'Mourning Our Astronauts: Public Commemoration after the Space Shuttle Tragedies,' paper delivered at the American Studies Association Annual Meeting, November 4, 2005, Washington, D.C.
30. For views on the challenges that spontaneous memorials pose for public institutions see, for example, James B. Gardner and Sarah M. Henry, 'September 11 and the Mourning After: Reflections on Collecting and Interpreting the History of Tragedy,' *The Public Historian* 24, no. 3 (Summer 2002), 37-52, and Michele V. Cloonan, 'Monumental Preservation: A Call to Action,' *American Libraries* (September 2004), 34-38.

European museums are also confronting these issues; see Margry, 'The Murder of Pim Fortuyn,' 113-114.

31. Sigmund Freud, 'Mourning and Melancholia,' *The Standard Edition of the Complete Psychological Works of Sigmund Freud*, trans. by James Strachey (London: Hogarth Press, 1974): volume 14, 243-258, quote p. 245.

32. George Hagman, 'Mourning: A Review and Reconsideration,' *International Journal of Psychoanalysis* 76 (October 1995), 909-925; Tammy Clewell, 'Mourning Beyond Melancholia: Freud's Psychoanalysis of Loss,' *Journal of the American Psychoanalytic Association* 52, no. 1 (Spring 2004), 43-67.

33. José E. Muñoz, 'Photographies of Mourning: Melancholia and Ambivalence' in Van Der Zee, Mapplethorpe, and 'Looking for Langston,' in Harry Stecopoulos and Michael Uebel, eds., *Race and the Subject of Masculinities* (Durham: Duke University Press, 1997), 355-356; see also Michael Moon, 'Memorial Rags,' in George E. Haggerty and Bonnie Zimmerman, eds., *Professions of Desire: Lesbian and Gay Studies in Literature* (NY: Modern Language Association, 1995), 233-240; Philip Novak, 'Circles and Circles of Sorrow: In the Wake of Morrison's *Sula*,' *PMLA* 114 (1999), 184-193; and Greg Forter, 'Against Melancholia: Contemporary Mourning Theory, Fitzgerald's *The Great Gatsby*, and the Politics of Unfinished Grief,' *differences* 14, no. 2 (2003), 134-170.

34. Phyllis R. Silverman and Dennis Klass, 'Introduction: What's the Problem?' in Klass, Silverman, and Steven L. Nickman, eds., *Continuing Bonds: New Understandings of Grief* (Washington D.C.: Taylor & Francis, 1996), 3-30, quote on p. 19.

35. The 'stage' or phase model stems from Elizabeth Kübler-Ross, who theorized the grieving process in terms of a progression from anger to bitterness and finally to acceptance; see *On Death and Dying* (New York: Macmillan, 1969).

36. Larry Beresford, 'Looking Back at Columbine,'in *Living With Grief, Coping with Public Tragedy*, Marcia Lattanzi-Licht and Kenneth J. Doka, eds. (New York: Brunner-Routledge, 2003), 46-47; Karen Daly, Principal, Martin Park Elementary School, Boulder, Colorado, Memo to parents, April 22, 1999; David Brown, 'Some Question Value of Trauma Sessions,' *Washington Post* (May 3, 1999), A-1.

37. Jerome Groopman, 'The Grief Industry,' *The New Yorker* (January 26, 2004), 45; on CISM see Louis A. Gamino, 'Critical Incident Stress Management and Other Crisis Counseling Approaches,' in *Living With Grief*, 123-138.

38. John R. Jordan and Robert A. Neimeyer, 'Does Grief Counseling Work?' *Death Studies* 27 (2003), 778; Marcia Lattanzi-Licht quoted in Beresford, 'Looking Back at Columbine,' 47; Christina Hoff Sommers and Sally Satel, *One Nation Under Therapy: How the Helping Culture is Eroding Self-Reliance* (New York: St. Martin's Press, 2005).

39. Arellano, 'Alma mia de tu alma,' in *Descanos: An Interrupted Journey*, 97.

40. Michael Warner, *Publics and Counterpublics* (New York: Zone Books, 2002), 177. In the Netherlands, there are two monuments, although not specifically 'national', to Dutch traffic deaths in general: in Rotterdam and Wassenaar. An annual remembrance day on the third Sunday in November commemorates these deaths with an empty row of chairs. In the village of Nuenen there is also a monument to young traffic deaths; see www.monument-nuenen.net/. Thanks to Peter Jan Margry for sharing this information with me.

41. The First International Symposium on Roadside Memorials was held at the University of New England, Armidale, New South Wales, Australia in June 2004. Publications on roadside shrines include those listed in notes 4 and 9; see also Jon K. Reid and Cynthia L. Reid, 'A Cross Marks the Spot: A Study of Roadside Death Memorials in Texas and Oklahoma,' *Death Studies* 25 (2001), 341-356, and Maida Owens, 'Louisiana Roadside Memorials: Negotiating an Emerging Tradition,' in Santino, *Spontaneous Shrines and the Public Memorialization of Death*, 119-145. For websites, see, for example http://www.roadsidememorial.org/; for online sales of roadside memorial crosses see http://roadsidememorials.com/index.html

42. Jennifer Clark and Majella Franzmann, 'Authority from Grief, Presence and Place in the Making of Roadside Memorials,' *Death Studies* 30, no. 6 (July 2006), 579-599.

43. See Michael D. Shear, 'Roadside Memorials Banned By VDOT,' *Washington Post* (February 21, 2003) B-1, and Ian Urbina, 'As Roadside Memorials Multiply, A Second Look,' *New York Times* (6 February 2006) A-1.

44. See the RoadPeace website at http://www.roadpeace.org/pr/index.html

45. Clinton quoted in Beresford, 'Looking Back at Columbine,' 42; Linenthal quoted in J. Morgan, 'Americans Leave Tokens of Grief at Murrah Building Blast Site,' *Boulder Daily Camera* (April 19, 1998), A-13.

46. Gail Holst-Warhaft, *The Cue for Passion: Grief and Its Political Uses* (Cambridge: Harvard University Press, 2000), 2.

47. Mervi Pantti, 'Masculine Tears, Feminine Tears – and Crocodile Tears: Mourning Olof Palme and Anna Lindh in Finnish Newspapers,' *Journalism* 6, no. 3 (2005), 357-377; see also Carolyn Kitch, '"Mourning in America": Ritual, Redemption, and Recovery in News Narrative After September 11,' *Journalism Studies* 4, no. 2 (2003), 213-224.

48. Robert Pogue Harrison, *The Dominion of the Dead* (Chicago: The University of Chicago Press, 2003), 57; see also Ernesto De Martino, *Morte e pianto rituale: Dal lamento funebre antico al pianto di Maria* (Turin: Bollati Boringhieri, 1975, reprint 2000), a cultural anthropology of mourning rituals in southern Italy in the late 1950s.

49. On the mass mediation of disaster and tragic death see, for example, Daniel Dayan and Elihu Katz, *Media Events: The Live Broadcasting of History* (Cambridge: Harvard University Press, 1994) and Nick Couldry, *Media Rituals: A Critical Approach* (London and New York: Routledge, 2003).

50. Timothy G. Ashplant, Graham Dawson, and Michael Roper, 'The Politics of War Memory and Commemoration: Contexts, Structures, and Dynamics,' in *The Politics of War Memory and Commemoration*, eds. Ashplant, Dawson, and Roper (London and New York: Routledge, 2000), 14. On Thomson's work see, for example, his *Anzac Memories: Living With the Legend* (New York: Oxford University Press, 1994), and 'Anzac Memories: Putting Popular Memory Theory into Practice in Australia', in *The Oral History Reader*, eds. Rob Perks and Alistair Thomson (New York: Routledge, 1998), 300-310.

51. David Simpson, *9/11: The Culture of Commemoration* (Chicago: University of Chicago Press, 2006), 156, 95. Simpson's reference to 'Taylorization' connotes the scientific management theories of Frederick Winslow Taylor, whose notions of industrial labor efficiency, motion studies, and worker management were widely adopted in the Progressive era and throughout the twentieth century.

52. William Gass, 'Monumentality/Mentality,' *Oppositions* 25 (Fall 1982), 129.

53. American Psychological Association, 'End-of-Life Care Issues,' at http://www.apa.org/pi/eol/historical.html, accessed June 17, 2003.

54. '2005 Wirthlin Report, A Study of American Attitudes Toward Ritualization and Memorialization,' (Mount Sterling, OH: Funeral and Memorial Information Council, 2005).

55. Robert A. Neimeyer, 'Research on Grief and Bereavement: Evolution and Revolution,' *Death Studies* 28, no. 6 (July-August 2004), 489.

56. See, for example, Jessica Mitford, *The American Way of Death* (New York: Random House, 1963), and Tony Walter, 'A New Model of Grief: Bereavement and Biography,' *Mortality* 1, no. 1 (1996), 7-25.

57. Cathy Caruth, 'Introduction,' in *Trauma: Explorations in Memory*, ed. Cathy Caruth (Baltimore: Johns Hopkins University Press, 1995), 4-5.

58. Georges Bataille, *Eroticism, Death and Sensuality* (San Francisco: City Light Books, 1986), 82.

59. Roland Barthes, *Camera Lucida: Reflections on Photography*, trans. Richard Howard (New York: Farrar, Straus and Giroux, Inc., 1981), 87.

60. Haney, Leimer, and Lowery, 'Spontaneous Memorialization,' 162.

61. On notions of the dead remaining persistently social creatures, see Lesley A. Sharp, *Strange Harvest: Organ Transplants, Denatured Bodies, and the Transformed Self* (Berkeley: University of California Press, 2006), 210 and passim.

62. Margry and Sánchez-Carretero, 'Memorializing Traumatic Death.' *Anthropology Today*.

63. Haney, Leimer, Lowerty, 'Spontaneous Memorialization,' 159-160.

64. Harrison, *The Dominion of the Dead*, 143-45; Zoe Crossland, 'Buried Lives: Forensic Archaeology and the Disappeared in Argentina,' *Archaeological Dialogues* 7, no. 2 (2000), 146-159.

65. Anthony DePalma, 'Illness Persisting in 9/11 Workers, Big Study Finds,' *New York Times* (September 6, 2006), A-1.

66. Shaila Dewan, 'Disasters and the Dead,' *New York Times* (16 October 2005) WK-4; Suzan Clarke, 'Families Remember WTC Victims, Fight for a Proper Burial,' *The Journal News* (October 18, 2005), at http://www.voicesofsept11.org/artman/publish/Fresh_Kills/article_002075. php# (accessed January 9, 2006). On remains found during construction of the World Trade Center, see David W. Dunlap, 'Road at Trade Center Site to Be Excavated for Remains,' *New York Times* (December 30, 2006): B-3.

67. C. J. Chivers, 'Lost at Sea Isn't What It Used to Be,' *New York Times* (November 14, 1999), Sect 4-16.

68. Michael Sledge, *Soldier Dead: How We Recover, Identity, Bury, and Honor Our Military Fallen* (New York: Columbia University Press, 2005), 33; James P. Delgado, 'Memorials, Myths and Symbols: The Significance of the ARIZONA Memorial,' *The Valley Forge Journal* 5, no. 4 (1991), 310-326; Edward Linenthal, *Sacred Ground: Americans and Their Battlefields*, 2nd ed. (Urbana and Chicago: University of Illinois Press, 1993), 173-212.

69. Katherine Verdery, *The Political Lives of Dead Bodies: Reburial and Postsocialist Change* (NY: Columbia University Press, 1999), 22-31.

70. Kerwin Lee Klein, 'On the Emergence of *Memory* in Historical Discourse,' *Representations* 69 (Winter 2000), 127-50; Barbie Zelizer, 'Reading the Past Against the Grain: The Shape of Memory Studies,' *Critical Studies in Mass Communication* 12, no. 2 (June 1995), 215-216; Jay Winter, 'The Generation of Memory: Reflections on the "Memory Boom" in Contemporary Historical Studies,' *GHI Bulletin* 27 (Fall 2000), 69-92. In an earlier essay, Charles Maier used the phrase 'memory industry' to describe Holocaust commemoration; see Charles S. Maier, 'A Surfeit of Memory? Reflections on History, Melancholy and Denial,' *History and Memory* 5, no. 2 (1993), 136-52.

71. Pierre Nora, *Les lieux de memoire* (Paris: Gallimard, 1984-92); Marita Sturken, 'The Remembering of Forgetting: Recovered Memory and the Question of Experience,' *Social Text* 57, no. 4 (Winter 1998), 103-125.

72. Nora, 'Between Memory and History,' 13; Juliet Mitchell, 'Memory and Psychoanalysis,' in Patricia Fara and Karalyn Patterson, eds., *Memory* (Cambridge: Cambridge University Press, 1998), 99. See also the influential work of cognitive psychologist Endel Tulving, such as *Elements of Episodic Memory* (Oxford: Oxford University Press, 1983).

73. Klein, 'On the Emergence of *Memory*,' 146.

74. Nora, 'Between Memory and History,' 8-9, 12.

75. Paul Ricoeur, *Memory, History, Forgetting*, trans. Kathleen Blamey and David Pellauer, (Chicago: University of Chicago Press, 2004 [2000]).

76. Roy Rosenzweig and David Thelen, *The Presence of the Past: Popular Uses of History in American Life* (New York: Columbia University Press, 1998).

77. Dominick LaCapra, *History in Transit: Experience, Identity, Critical Theory* (Ithaca: Cornell University Press, 2004), 3 and passim.

78. See the National Civil Rights Museum website at http://www.civilrightsmuseum.org/gallery/rooms306_307.asp; accessed September 15, 2006. The museum's claims are not quite accurate: the room where King stayed was demolished and then reconfigured in order to permit museum visitor visibility; see Mabel O. Wilson, 'Between Rooms 307: Spaces of Memory at the National Civil Rights Museum,' in Craig Evan Barton, ed., *Sites of Memory: Perspectives on Architecture and Race* (New York: Princeton Architectural Press, 2001), 23-24.

79. Alison Landsberg, *Prosthetic Memory: The Transformation of American Remembrance in the Age of Mass Culture* (New York: Columbia University Press, 2004), 2.

80. Joan W. Scott, 'The Evidence of Experience,' *Critical Inquiry* 17, no. 4 (Summer 1991), 779.

81. Carole Blair, 'Contemporary U.S. Memorial Sites as Exemplar's of Rhetoric's Materiality,' in Jack Selzer and Sharon Crowley, *Rhetorical Bodies* (Madison: University of Wisconsin Press, 1999), 46.

82. C. Nadia Seremetakis, ed., *The Senses Still: Perception and Memory As Material Culture in Modernity* (Chicago: The University of Chicago Press, 1994), 9; see also Paul Connerton, *How Societies Remember* (Cambridge: Cambridge University Press, 1989) and Christopher Pinney's discussion of 'corpothetics,' or 'the sensory embrace of images' in *Beyond Aesthetics: Art and the Technologies of Enchantment*, eds. Christopher Pinney and Nicholas Thomas (Oxford: Berg, 2001), 158.

83. P. West, *Conspicuous Compassion: Why Sometimes It Is Really Cruel to Be Kind* (London: Civitas, 2004), as noted in Pantti, 'Masculine Tears,' 357.

84. Kate V. Hartig and Kevin M. Dunn, 'Roadside Memorials: Interpreting New Deathscapes in Newcastle, New South Wales,' *Australian Geographical Studies* 36, no. 1 (March 1998), 5-20; Erika Doss, 'Spontaneous Memorials and Contemporary Modes of Mourning in America,' *Material Religion: The Journal of Objects, Art, and Belief* 2, no. 3 (November 2006), 294-318.

St. Francis College Library

180 Remsen Street
Brooklyn, NY 11201

CPSIA information can be obtained
at www.ICGtesting.com
Printed in the USA
LVOW13s0052251017

553662LV00002B/40/P